52+ WAYS TO FILL YOUR BEDS AND GROW YOUR CARE SERVICE

ATTENTION CARE-HOME AND HOME-CARE OWNERS AND MANAGERS

MORE PROFITS – MORE TIME – MORE FREEDOM

GEOFFREY FAIRFIELD

Book Design by HMDpublishing

Paperback: 978-1-7396710-0-6

E-book: 978-1-7396710-1-3

DEDICATION

This book is dedicated to my wife Janice who has supported me over many years and without whom, it probably would not have happened.

I am also dedicating it to you, the reader. Let it be a guide to help you on your road to success.

CONTENTS

INTRODUCTION

Congratulations.

If you have this book in your hands, that means that you are passionate about your care home or home-care service, and you want to take it to the next level.

This book is comprised of a series of marketing tips and ideas that were originally published in the Care Managers Hub Facebook group.

You can simply read through the book or just dip in and out of it whenever you find that you need some inspiration to improve the marketing of your care service.

You will find tips, ideas and inspirations that are not generally used by most care services. That means that, if you put some of these ideas into action, you will be way ahead of your competitors.

For many of the items, you will be able to find checklists and templates that you can download from the Care Managers Hub. See the end section of the book for more information.

Be sure to take a look at the section on how you can find more service users without any marketing costs.

Finding staff is a problem for many and so I have included a section at the end which I hope will be of help.

Avoid the huge mistakes that many care services are doing. Put these ideas into practice and see the benefits for yourselves.

What Marketing is All About

If you find marketing complicated, here is a simple summary of what it's all about...

"Expose your business to the right people, more often".

This means that if you want to find more service users, you need to be telling the right people that could use your service. You need to be telling those people as frequently as you can all about your service and why it is right for them.

So how can you do the 'telling'?

Advertising, PR (news stories to the press), social media etc. This is where you may need expert help. There are many companies who will be only too willing to help you and many that specialise in the care market.

Who are the 'right people'? You need to have defined your target market group. This could be by age, by disability type, by area, by profession or something else. When you have defined your ideal market group it will make your marketing so much easier.

The more you can do, the more chances you will have of finding more service users. So, you need to plan your time to ensure that this important part of your work does not get overlooked. So how can you increase the amount of exposure you are getting? Make a plan...

What Makes You Stand Out From the Crowd?

Do you know your USPs?

Your USPs are your Unique Selling Points. They are what makes your care service or care home stand out from the crowd- why someone should choose you rather than one of your competitors.

If you are not clear on what your USP's are there is an excellent checklist you can download from the Care Managers Hub. This is just so important- if you aren't clear on what makes you different or better than your competitors, why do you think any prospective service user would choose you?

Once you are clear on what your USPs are, you need to be telling the world about them at every possible moment- in other words you need to be mentioning them in all of your marketing- on your website, in brochures, in social media posts etc.

Even if you think your competitors have the same facilities as you do, don't be afraid to shout out about it.

Quite simply- he who shouts the loudest gets noticed.

Have You Set Your Marketing Goals?

December and January is the time of year to be thinking about goal setting- but what about your marketing goals? What do you want to achieve?

Do you want to find more service users? You need to be specific- so how many exactly to you want to find?

What about additional staff? You can use your marketing for that also. How many more staff do you need?

Once you know exactly what you need, you can then start to make your plans. But you need to be really clear and specific about what you want.

Go on, get started with your plans and remember to get really clear first.

How Often do You do Marketing?

Whether you are looking for more staff or more service users, you need to use your best marketing techniques in order to find the people you need.

It doesn't matter if you are posting in social media, sending emails, advertising on bulletin boards or in the newspaper, sending out press releases or anything else you do. If you just do it once, it won't work.

Why do we keep seeing the adverts on TV again and again? It's because repetition works.

To get the best from any marketing you do, you need to be repeating it regularly.

Does this sound like a lot of work? Can you automate it? There are a lot of apps available which allow you to set it up and then leave it to run automatically.

If that sounds too much for you, then why not delegate it to someone else? If you don't have anyone else, then look at sites like Fiverr.com or upwork.com.

So, if you need more staff or service users, make a plan for your marketing to happen on a regular basis.

How Important is Marketing to You?

If you need more service users, and you need them urgently, here is one thing you can do...

Make sure that you are focussing your time on this. Check your to-do list. How many of your actions are all about marketing or sales?

Is it at the top of your list?

Can you do at least one thing every day which will move you forward to finding new people that would love to join your care service?

Getting Better at Marketing

You probably spend quite a lot of time and money in training people in all aspects of care.

But what about sales and marketing? Does that ever get any attention?

Here are some things you and your team could get better at:

- Converting the enquiries you get into sales
- Following up with enquiries
- Writing adverts and press releases
- Improving your website
- Using social media to get more enquiries
- And much more...

The good news is that all of these things are can be learned. There are many training courses available. I urge you to give priority to these items if you are looking for more service users.

Understand the Life-Time Value of a Client

When considering your marketing, it's important to know how much a service user is worth to you. You can also look at it another way- If your home or your portfolio is not full, how much money are you losing?

Let's look at an example...

Let's say you earn £1,000 a week from a service user. I know it may me more and it may be less, depending on various factors such as where you are in the country and the type of service you are offering etc. but this will give you an idea.

£1,000 per week is £52,000 per year.

Let's say that service users stay with you for an average of 3 years, then each one is worth £52,000 x 3 or £156,000! Wow!

If you need 5 service users, then the total is £156,000 x 5 or £780,000!

So, how much should you spend on marketing. Would it be worth spending £1,000, £5,000 or £10,000?

So, if you are reluctant to spend money on marketing, just realise the benefit that this could bring for you.

How Much Should You Spend on Marketing?

How much should you spend on marketing to get new service users?

Remember in the previous tip that the lifetime value of a client could be £156,000.

Your own figures may differ from that, but the principle still holds true.

So how much would you spend to get in £156,000?

If I could give you a new enquiry for your care service, how much would you pay me? £50, £500, £1,000, £5,000 or more?

If you invested say £1,000 per month to get in say 5 leads, would that be worth it?

Well the answer is- it depends.

It depends on a number of things such as the quality of the leads, how quickly you follow up and how well you follow up to close the deal.

The only way you can know is to closely monitor the results... and keep improving on what you do.

All I can say is... if you do not spend anything on marketing you may get no enquiries at all.

My suggestion would be that, before you start spending money on marketing, try using many of the free ways of gaining leads... more on that later.

Go on... get started today.

Your Ideal Client

We all know that marketing can be VERY expensive.

Advertising can be like throwing mud against the wall and hoping that some of it sticks.

Before you do any marketing, it is essential to be really clear about who your ideal client or 'avatar' is. There are some care services that specialise in niche markets as diverse as former military personnel, freemasons or musicians.

These will therefore easily be able to precisely target their marketing. They will know where to direct their messages and will know what kind of language to use in their messages. Also, their service users will have something in common with each other and therefore will have a more pleasant experience together.

In the Care Managers Hub you can download a template to help you find your ideal customer.

This is just one of the many important pieces that you need to have in place in order to attract new service users and staff.

What to do if You Don't Have the Time?

Do you need more service users?

You need to do more marketing, but you don't really have the time as your priority is looking after your existing clients?

Not doing any marketing is a risk that you can't really afford to take. So, what is the answer?

You need to outsource the marketing.

You can either outsource the whole of your marketing or just parts of it. There are marketing companies who specialise in the care sector. They will help you create a marketing plan and do as much of your marketing as you want them to and will work within your own budget.

There are also specialist companies who focus on specific areas such as digital marketing, PR or website design and search engine optimisation (SEO).

You could also look at using individual people who will perform specific tasks for you such as designing a web page or creating a sales letter.

Places you can go to find the help you need include Fiverr.com and Elance.com. On the sites, people will bid to do the work for you and you can then choose the one you like best.

If you are not doing any regular marketing, then I urge you to get started today. If you are already doing something, then see what more you can do.

Do it Yourself or Get Help In?

We all know that in order to find more service users and more staff, we need to be doing more marketing.

But the question is... should we be doing it ourselves or putting it out for others to do... or perhaps a mixture of the two?

Well, here are some points for you to think about...

Doing it Ourselves

- Great if you have the skills- you need to know what you are doing
- Can save you loads of money
- Can be quite time-consuming
- Keeps it within your control
- You may not get the same results as using a specialist

Using Help from Expert Companies

- Will help you get better results and a more professional appearance
- Will save you loads of time and allow you to focus on the other really important tasks you need to be doing
- Will probably get it done quicker than if you do it yourself
- You need to be able to afford the cost

You will need to look at different areas of marketing separately. For example, you may need help with website design or Google advertising but you may be fine with doing your own PR.

You need to assess your own strengths and then use the above lists to decide what is best for you.

USING YOUR WEBSITE

How Often do You Update Your Website?

If you want your website to be found by search engines such as Google, one of the things you need to do is to update it regularly. with new, fresh information.

These could be good news stories showing happy service users or details of new services you are offering.

You need to find someone to delegate this to and set up regular reminders so that this does not get overlooked.

Go on... get started today.

Using Your Website to Generate Enquiries

Here are some thoughts and ideas for you to help you improve in generating enquiries for your care service.

- Make the buttons on the site in contrasting colours.
- Don't use 'Submit'. Instead use something like 'Send for your free guide'.
- 10% rule- on average only around 10% of people read a website, so highlight the important points.
- Make the website responsive. Check it out on different devices.
- Use A/B testing to improve the site.
- Test the speed of the website at https://tools.pingdom.com/.
- Tracking- can you track where your enquiries come from?
- Put a chat system on the site- see www.tidio.com.
- Social proof is important- use testimonials, case studies etc

- Make sure the website has clear sections.
- Avoid reversed out text such as black on white.

Check Your Website for Reversed-out Text

Do you use reversed-out text? Standard text is black text on a white background. Reversed-out text is white text on a black or dark-coloured background.

Did you realise that reversed-out text is not a good thing to use. Why?

White reversed-out text has a disastrous impact on reader comprehension. Tests were done with getting people to read black text on white and then testing their comprehension. The same tests were then done with a different group of people but with white text on black.

In the first case, 70% of people had good comprehension but with reversed-out text good comprehension fell to 0% and only 12% of people having fair comprehension. What a difference!

Please check your websites and, if you have any reversed-out text, change it to get the best responses from your websites.

Make It Easy for People to Get in Touch

I am sure we would all agree that a key goal of our website is to find new service users.

One thing you must therefore be doing is to make it as easy as possible for people to get in touch with you. Here are few ideas for you…

1. How easy is it for people to find your phone number? Have it clearly visible at the top of EVERY page.

2. You need to capture the details of as many people as possible of those who are browsing your site. Have a 'lead capture form' where people can leave their name, email and phone number. Again, if possible, put this on EVERY page.

3. Have a 'lead magnet'. This is a document that people can download in return for providing their information. These could include a brochure, a checklist, an e-book or a quiz. If you use an email system, all of this can be automated.

The 'About Us' Page

Here are the top 6 things people look for on a website:

1. Products or services

2. Contact information

3. The 'About Us' page

4. Testimonials

5. Blog

6. Pricing

The 'About Us' page is so very important. Here are some tips to make this page work for you:

○ Make it about the customer- not about you

○ Talk TO your customers not AT them. In other words, don't preach, use your normal tone of voice.

○ Tell your story- this will really help to engage people.

○ Don't just say it- show it. Add visual images to really grab people's attention.

○ Liking- people like people that are like them. Share personal information.

SOCIAL MEDIA ADVERTISING

Google Advertising

If someone is looking for a care home or a care provider, what do they do? They go to Google and they may type something like "care home in ___". When they do that it's like they are holding up their hand and saying I'm a prospective use of your service.

The problem is that you can't guarantee that your website will appear near the top of the listing, or even on the first page.

So, this week I am going to talk about Google advertising. It's a way of ensuring that your advert will appear depending on the keywords that someone types in. The good news however is that you pay only when someone clicks on your advert and then gets taken to your website or landing page.

You might think that advertising is expensive but it's you who sets the budget at how much you spend. If you want to spend only £10 per day for example, then Google will restrict it to that. So, you can start off very inexpensively.

Using Social Media Advertising to Find More Clients

In order to find more service users, you could use Google or Facebook advertising. You will only ever spend as much as you want to... and you can start off small- £5 a day if you wish.

You will only pay when someone clicks on your advert. So a key metric you need to be monitoring is 'Cost per Click' or CPC. The aim is to keep this as low as possible. You can do this by testing different keywords that are used in your advert. Keep experimenting to drive your CPC lower.

Reducing the Cost of Social Media Advertising

Previously, I mentioned that you need to be aiming to continually reduce your Cost per Click (CPC) when using Google of Facebook advertising.

This will depend on the key words that you use. The more popular the key word, the more expensive it will be.

Less popular key words will have less competition, so you may find your ad appearing nearer the top of the search results. So for example- the term 'care home' may be expensive but 'outstanding care home in Bognor Regis' will be far less expensive. Also, with the latter, you will get more targeted and relevant results.

This subject can be complicated and we recommend that you get the help of expert companies who will look after it for you.

Making Social Media Work For You

Following on from the last tip, I will continue with Google or Facebook advertising. When people click on your advert, they will be taken to your website or a specially designed 'landing page'. The objective is for you to get their details, or otherwise you have wasted your money.

You need an enquiry form where people can enter their name, email address and possibly their phone number.

Often, it's a good idea to give people an incentive for giving you their details. This could be something like a brochure or an e-book which they can download once they have given you their information.

MARKETING FOR FREE (OR WITH VERY LITTLE COST)

The next three sections, Social Media, P.R. and Testimonials will show you ways of marketing on a low budget.

Good News

You can certainly advertise in Google, Facebook and many more but how can you find new service users without it costing you a penny?

The answer is very simple. Post good news stories about what is happening in your care service. Has someone had a special birthday? Have your residents been on a day trip or completed some interesting activities? Have you started a new service?

You can post on your own page, but if you don't have many followers, then not many people will see it.

Here's a suggestion for you. Join a local Facebook group and post in there. The post will then be seen by many people in your local area. Post on a regular basis and you will get a reputation for being a care service that is proactive, caring and successful.

Make It Regular

Do you use Facebook, LinkedIn, Instagram or Twitter? If not, you are missing out on a great way to find more service users.

Posting on a regular basis is a must. But when you do, make sure that people have an easy way for people to contact you. Is your phone number, your email address or your website information clearly visible? If possible, have a link to a page where there is a form where you can capture people's email addresses and/or phone numbers.

Go on... get started today.

What to Post on Social Media

One of the best ways to find new service users is to use Social Media- the most popular places are probably Facebook, Instagram, Twitter and LinkedIn.

But what should you post?

What everyone is looking for are 'good news stories'. So here are a few ideas for you:

- Care homes reopening to families of residents
- Residents birthday celebrations
- Visits from celebrities
- Unusual activities- for example- Easter celebrations
- Staff length of service celebrations
- Refurbishments in the home
- Arts and crafts activities
- People generally enjoying themselves

What other ideas can you think of?

Using P.R.- Marketing for Free

Unlike using paid advertising, using P.R. is an almost free way of creating publicity for your care service.

Firstly, what is it?

In simple terms, it's getting information about your care service out to the general public in a way that will attract them and get them to take action to contact you.

In practice, this means writing a press release or story about something interesting that has happened and posting that in social media and sending it out to newspapers, magazines, TV, radio and anyone else who may be able to publicise your information.

A picture is worth a thousand words, so make sure you include at least one picture. Make sure this is in a high-resolution format if it is going to be printed.

Although generally free, there may be a small charge if things are going to be printed.

If you don't have time to do this, get someone in to help you. P.R. is not just for finding new service users. You can also use it to find staff.

Using P.R. to Find More Service Users

PR is something you can do to help you find more service users that will not necessarily cost anything, other than some of your time.

The simple way to do this is to find news stories, especially good news stories, and send them out to the local press, TV, radio, magazines, etc..

So, firstly create an email list.

So make sure that you are regularly taking pictures of events that are going on with your service users. Then write up a short story about what is happening and send it out to the list.

If writing is not your strong point, ask around and see if any of your staff would like to take up that role. You may well find an undiscovered star amongst your team.

Now is the time to do this. The press is desperate for good news stories.

Lessons From 'The Greatest Showman'

Do you use PR to find new service users?

Whereas advertising is costly, using PR can be free or very low cost. So what is it?

If you have seen the movie The Greatest Showman, you will remember P.T. Barnum riding through the town on the back of an elephant. Barnum was extremely smart and knew the benefit that the exposure would give him.

So how does this relate to me? You may well ask. No, you don't need to go out and buy an elephant. It's about thinking about how you can use resources that you already have to gain more exposure for your care service. Here are just a few ideas:

- Send stories to your local press, TV and radio stations

- Contact local old people's clubs

- Host tea parties or coffee mornings (when allowed) for lonely people in your community

- Take a stall at local fete or exhibition

- Put up posters in local shops, libraries etc
- Put your branding on any vehicles you have including contact information
- Sponsor a local football team
- Contact relevant charities in your area.

Why not organise a brainstorming session with your staff and see what ideas they can come up with- you may just be surprised.

Go on- give it a go. Your care service will really benefit from this.

Using Testimonials in Your Marketing

Do you get testimonials and use them in your marketing?

These are positive stories and comments about the service you provide that you can use on your website, brochures, newsletters, emails and anywhere else that is seen by people outside of your service.

Make this a standard part of your routine. You can get testimonials from your service users and their family members. Just ask them what they like about the service you are providing.

As you sign up a new service user, tell them: "We hope you will be very happy with us. Later on we will be coming to you and asking you for a testimonial. Is that ok with you?".

At that point they are unlikely to refuse, and you have created the anticipation that you will be asking later.

Put a reminder into your system and then do it.

Remember then to add the testimonial in appropriate places.

Do You Get Testimonials?

I previously mentioned about the importance of testimonials and using them in your marketing.

In order to make this work, you need a central place where all testimonials are stored.

For written testimonials such as letters, use a standard file or folder to keep this in a safe place.

For digital testimonials such as emails or comments in social media, you need a place where you can easily copy and paste these to. Personally, I use a page in Evernote where it is super-easy to find these whenever I need to.

Make sure that, whatever you use, it is a place that can be easily shared with anyone who gets involved with the marketing and may need to use the testimonials.

FOLLOWING UP

Do You Follow-up?

I am sure you have had many enquiries for your care home or home-care service when, after talking to them, they have told you 'We are not ready to make a decision yet' or 'I am just making enquiries'.

What do you do with those names? Do you have a follow-up system?

Ideally this would be some kind of system such as Mailchimp or PipeDrive. This system would remind you to follow-up by phone or send automated emails to them.

You could also use a simple spreadsheet. The key thing is to record their details and then have a simple system to remind you to follow-up.

Whether you follow up by phone, email or something else, the key is to follow up and keep in touch with them.

If you don't do this, they will be contacted by care services that do follow-up.

Go on, can you give this a go?

How Often Do You Follow up?

How often do you follow-up with any enquiries from prospective service users?

We all know that anyone looking for a care service will not just come to you. They will be shopping around and making enquiries at a number of places.

So you need to be following up promptly and regularly, otherwise your competitors will get there ahead of you.

You can follow up by phone, email, text message and any other way that you have of keeping in touch. It doesn't really matter as long as you keep your service at the top of their mind so that when they are ready to go ahead they will think of you.

But you need a system... Depending on how you like to work, this could be a note in your diary to call someone, you could delegate it to someone else to call them on a regular basis. or you could set up an autoresponder system to send out emails every so often. Decide what you are going to do and then put in a system which works for you.

KNOWING
YOUR RESULTS

Knowing Your Results

Do you know how well your website is doing?

Firstly, you need to decide what it's meant to be doing. What do you want it to do for you?

- Find new service users
- Find new staff
- Promote your brand/image
- Provide information
- Keep people informed
- Something else

Whatever it is that you want your website to be doing, you need to be clear on what results you would like to expect.

You therefore need to measure your results. You need to know what is working and what isn't.

Then you need to stop what isn't working and do more of what is.

But be specific- for example, if your goal is to find new service users, how many are you getting each month? If you are not getting many, at least measure how many new enquiries you are getting.

Whatever it is, start measuring your results now, and start improving.

Measure Your Results

If you want to find new service users, you may have allocated a certain portion of your annual budget towards that.

So you need to know what is working and what is not. In other words, you need to be measuring your results. But where to start...?

Firstly, record the amount you have spent on advertising or any other forms of marketing.

Secondly, record the number of enquiries you receive for your care service and note the source next to each enquiry. By source, I mean was it a recommendation, was it from Facebook or from somewhere else? You can do this using a simple spreadsheet to start with.

Divide the cost spent by the number of enquiries- that will give a cost per lead figure. Aim to reduce that each month.

Analyse which lead sources produce the best results for you and focus your money and attention in these areas?

Next, record how many confirmed new service users you are getting each month. Work out the percentage success rate you are getting from your enquiries... and aim to improve.

These are the minimum figures you need to be focussing on. Produce a monthly report to review each month.

Obviously, you can produce much more detailed reports if you wish. But that's for another time...

Measure for Success

You have probably heard the old adage that 50% of advertising works successfully. The trouble is that we don't know which 50%.

The key to success on marketing and getting the best results from the valuable £££s you are spending is to measure your results so that you can find out which activities give you the best results.

For example, if you just measure the number of enquiries you receive, you can find out if advertising in journal A gets better results than advertising on website B or posting in Facebook does better than posting on Twitter.

But that is just the start.

In marketing there are hundreds of things that can be measured and I will cover more on that another time.

For now, just start recording each enquiry you get and where it came from.

After only around 2-3 months, you will start to get an idea of where the best results are coming from.

GENERAL
TIPS AND IDEAS

Your Google Business Page

When someone does a search in Google, after all the adverts you will see a map and three businesses.

This area gets lots of clicks and so you need to make sure that your business is featured there. Do a search such as 'care home in xxx' and see if your care service is featured.

Google gives your business a business page that you can manage yourself.

You can customise the page with photos and videos. Make sure that your website, phone number etc is correct.

What About Your Prices?

When did you last increase your prices? Has it been a while?

Do you think that, in the current economic climate that you can't increase your prices?

If you rely totally on clients from social services then you may not be able to raise your prices.

Well, have a think about this? How many people have turned your service down because you were too expensive? You will probably find that it's not many at all.

So could you do this... increase your prices by say 1%, or 2% or 3%?

If you did increase your prices, would you really lose clients? I suspect not.

Those 1%'s add up and at the end of the year will provide some extremely useful additional income.

In marketing, it's all about testing. So why not do a trial and raise your prices for new service users for just one month. Measure the results you get and see if this works for you.

Your Domain Name

Your domain name is so important to help you find new service users and staff.

In case you are not familiar with the term 'domain name', it is the name that people use to find your service on the internet. This usually starts with www and is something like www.diamondcare.co.uk (a made-up name).

If the name of your care service is Diamond Care, then you certainly will want to register the above name.

But have you thought that most people will not be searching for 'Diamond Care'? They will probably be searching for something like 'care home in Torquay', domiciliary care in Nantwich or 'nursing home in Glasgow'.

So why not consider registering the domain names of www. torquaycarehome.co.uk, www.nantwichdomiciliarycare. co.uk or www.glasgownursinghome.co.uk. You can do any variations on this. I'm sure you get the idea anyway.

When anyone types those search terms into Google you should come out near the top. If you want your care service to get found, this could be a quick and simple thing to do. You can still keep your existing domain name and both domains will point to your existing website.

Domain names are very inexpensive to register, so why not get started today.

Your Phone Number

Did you know that you can analyse who is looking at your website?

There are tools such as Google Analytics which will give you a fantastic amount of information about where your enquiries are coming from.

Information is power, and so, if you know for example that you are getting many enquiries from one site, you can direct more of your advertising there.

However, when someone phones you, it's not possible to analyse how they got your details and where they are calling from... or is it?

Are they calling from an online advert, a social media post, your website, Linkedin, a blog post or something else?

Now you <u>can</u> find out. There are digital systems available which will create a dynamic phone number on your website. When someone uses that phone number, the system records exactly where they have come from, allowing you to track the calls.

There are many systems available but one you could look at is <u>https://www.responsetap.com/gb/</u>. Have a look and see if that could work for you.

Split-Testing for Success

Do you use social media to find new service users and care staff? Do you advertise in Google or Facebook?

We all know that whatever you do, you need to be measuring the results in order to continually improve the results you are getting and therefore the return you are getting on your investment.

What I want to mention is the concept of 'split-testing'. This is where you would generally post two or more different versions of your advert in order to see which is best. The changes you make could be quite subtle- a change in the headline, different colours, different fonts or different wording.

The changes you make may be quite subtle- maybe just one word in the headline, for example. But that one word can make all the difference to the results you get.

You can also use split testing in mail shots. You can send out different versions to segments of your mailing list, find out which one works best and then send the best one to the remainder of your list.

There are lots of different ways you can use this concept. Marketing is all about trial and testing. See what works for you and then continually improve on that.

Asking For Referrals

If you need more service users, and you need them urgently, here is one thing you can do...

Ask for referrals?

A referral is a recommendation from one of your service users or their families and friends to someone else who may be considering the same type of service. Referrals cost you nothing, other than some of your time, but you do need a system to make it happen.

Simply, every time you get a new service user, ask them "Do you have any family or friends who may be interested in this type of service?" Ask them if they will give you the names of those people.

The best time to ask will be after someone has settled in. Ask them if they are happy with what you are doing for them. Only when you get a positive response, then ask for the referral.

Be Different in Order to Get Noticed

If you need more service users, and you need them urgently, here is one thing you can do...

Stand out - be different.

If the image of your care service is the same as everyone else you will not be noticed. So, if you want more service users you need to highlight what makes you different from other care services.

There are many ways of 'being different'. Here are just a few ideas.

Does your service specialise in anything? Do you cater for a particular type of service-user such as ex-servicemen, musicians, freemasons etc? Having a niche like that makes you stand out, particularly to those people who fall into that category.

Do you offer anything that other services do not? This could be things like special types of treatment, cordon bleu food, visits to museums etc etc.

Take the time out to sit down and brainstorm in what ways your service is different or in what ways you could make it different. And then market it as fully as you can. The more you can make people aware, the more you will get seen and the more your care service will benefit.

Can you do at least one thing every day which will move you forward to finding new people that would love to join your care service?

Ways of Increasing Your Income

If you thought there was only one way of increasing your income, then read on...

1. **Get more service users**- it sounds obvious doesn't it? Whether you are in a care home or in domiciliary care, this has to be a major focus for you. In a care home you are limited by the number of beds available but in domiciliary care there is no limit to the number of service users you could effectively take on. Either way, this has to be a major focus for you. You can find a checklist you can download in the Care Managers Hub.

2. **Increase your prices**- Have you recently checked to see what your competition are charging? What about a 1% increase? Would you really lose business? what about a 2 or 3% increase? What about 10% or 15%?

3. **Offer more services**- What other services could you offer? If you run out of ideas, take a look at the websites of your competitors. What are they doing that you could copy?

4. **Check your retention**- Particularly in domiciliary care, are people stopping using your services when you are not expecting them to? Find out what is going on. Are you providing poor service or is it some other reason? What can you do to improve?

Nelson's Column or the Acropolis?

How many ways do you have of attracting new service users?

If you have just one, then you are leaving yourself in a very dangerous situation.

If something happens with that, then you are leaving your organisation exposed. You are like Nelson's Column- with just one leg.

If you think that things won't go wrong, then think again- the internet can go down, your key contacts can leave, Facebook can cancel your account, your computers can get hacked etc etc.

Do you really want to risk being in this situation? If your enquiries dry up, then you could be in trouble.

It's much better to be like the Acropolis with many supports. If you have many different ways of finding new service users then you are protecting yourself in case anything should happen to one of those.

Are you like Nelson's Column or like the Acropolis?

What other ways can you think of for attracting new service users?

What Does Your Brand Say About You?

Does your care service have a brand?

In order to stand out from your competitors, you need to have a strong brand.

Here are some key pointers for you to consider:

- Define your brand- What are your values and beliefs?
- Identify your strengths - Why should people use your care service instead of your competitors?
- Know your target audience - Who do you want to reach with your services? Can you narrow it down to a unique niche? How and where can you reach these people?
- Create your brand story - How do you tell people what you do and why you do it?
- Find your voice - What tone do you use to connect with your audience?

- Design your look - How do you represent yourself visually? Does your aesthetic communicate your story and your values?

- Be consistent - Is your branding consistent across all your platforms?

Take some time out with your key people and go through this checklist. Even if you already do marketing, this will be a great refresher for all.

Check on Your Image

If you have a care home or an office, what does it say about you from the outside? Does it portray the image that you would like it to?

Is it well kept and well presented? Do you feel proud of it?

Do you have signage that gives out the appropriate message? If you are on a street with passing traffic, this is a golden opportunity to attract new service providers?

Remember, you only get one opportunity to make a first impression. Go on, go outside now and do a check for things that could be improved.

If you want to be 'outstanding', then you need to be outstanding from the outside also.

Who Answers the Phone?

It is obvious that when someone calls you to enquire about your service that a) the phone needs to be answered promptly and b) it needs to be answered by someone who has ideally been trained in sales and understands all about the service you are offering or at least can take all the relevant information as a message.

So let me ask you... who answers the phone during the day?

Is it someone who has been properly trained in sales or at least to take messages?

But what happens after hours? Do the phones just ring, or do you have an answering machine? Alternatively, are the phones answered by a carer or someone who has not been trained?

In either of these scenarios, you could be losing out.

If you have an enquiry from a potential new service user and it is not dealt with promptly and efficiently, then it is the equivalent of just throwing money down the drain, especially if you have been spending money on marketing.

So how do you deal with calls in the evening and at the weekend?

Here's an idea that you may not have thought of. Use a professionally trained answering service. They will be able to answer basic questions about your service and take all the details and information for you to respond to.

These services are quite inexpensive these days. They are well organised and will give a professional appearance to your service. They will also stop interruptions and, if you are in a care home, allow carers to do what they are meant to be doing.

Speed Stuns!

if you get an enquiry for your care service, there is nothing more that will impress your potential service user than responding to them quickly- the quicker the better.

Yes, speed really does stun!

There are a number of reasons for this.

Firstly, they will be impressed at just how efficient you are.

Next, you will be ahead of your competitors. If you can get in first and arrange a home visit before anyone else, you will be well ahead in the game.

So, review the different types of enquiries you receive and how quickly you respond.

Go on... stun your potential service users with just how quick you can be.

Are You Shouting?

What do you mean Geoff?

If you need more service users, quite simply you need to shout about it... not literally, of course.

But you need to be shouting about it whenever and whereever you can.

That's why you keep seeing the same TV ads over and over again. It's because it takes repetition to get the message across.

Your goal is to create 'top of mind awareness'.

If I said to you 'Name a burger company...', chances are you would say McDonalds. Why? It's because of all the advertising they have done.

So if you said to someone- 'Name a care-home or home-care service', would they think of your service?

So, the key is to get your message out in as many places as possible. It doesn't mean you have to spend a fortune on advertising. There are many free ways of getting your name across- social media is just one.

So, if you are looking for more service users, sit down and make a list of all the places where you could be getting your name across.

By the way, there is a check list you can download in the Care Managers Hub.

Choose the areas you want to focus on, the ones that you think will have the best chance of finding the ideal people for your service.

Then brainstorm ways of getting your name out there, over and over again, so that people will start to remember you.

If you need more service users, give this a go.

Do You Ask Good Questions?

This is about asking questions...

Why should I ask questions? Now that's a good question.

By asking questions you can learn so much about your care service and how to improve it so that you can get more service users.

The answers to the questions will also help you creating your marketing or, for example, what to say on your website.

So, here are a few questions you could be asking:

1. What do you like about our care service? You can even get more specific with questions like:

    ○ What do you like about our staff?

    ○ What do you like about our food?

- What do you like about your accommodation?
- What do you like about the activities?
- etc etc.

2. What could be improved? Again, you can get specific with more detailed questions.

3. Why did you choose our care service?

4. If you were to recommend us to others, what are the key things that you would tell them about?

So, who can you ask these questions to?

- Well firstly of course, your current service users.
- The families of the service users
- Previous service users
- Your staff
- Care home visitors

After you start asking these questions, you will start to see a pattern emerging.

Hopefully, the answers will not be a surprise to you, but you may get some new angles on things that you hadn't previously thought about.

You can then start using this information to create marketing messages on your website, in emails, newsletters, social media etc.

Using a Lead Magnet to Attract More Service Users

Do you have a lead magnet? Firstly, let me explain what I am talking about.

We all know how important it is to have a good website and how important it is to get people to come and look at your website.

Well, that's all very well, but when people come to the website, we want them to take some action- ideally either picking up the phone to call you or filling in a form to request further information.

The key is to give them an incentive to fill in that form in order to contact you. Once you have their contact details you will be in a position to follow up and contact them with a view to possible signing them up for your care service.

The lead magnet is something you will offer your prospective customer as an incentive for filling in your form. If they fill in your form to get your lead magnet they are effectively sending you a signal that they are a prospective customer.

Here are some examples of what you could use as a lead magnet:

- A brochure with information about your care service
- A checklist of something useful e.g. '7 Steps to Choosing Your Ideal Care Service'.
- A whitepaper
- A report
- A tips booklet
- A video or dvd
- A quiz or survey

All these items can be accessed once someone has filled in the form.

These items will really help to increase the number of people who fill in your forms.

Your Email Signature

What's in your email signature?

An email signature is what comes after your name at the bottom of your email.

Every email you send is an opportunity to market yourself and your care service. So if you're just putting your name and contact details then you are not taking full advantage of the opportunity to engage and connect with the people you are emailing.

So what should go in your signature? Much of this will depend on your personal preference and your organisation's brand and culture. However, here are a few suggestions for you:

- First and last name
- Job title
- Secondary contact information
- Social media icons with links
- A call to action e.g click here to get our latest brochure
- Booking links- e.g. click here to come and view our home
- Industry disclaimer or legal requirements
- Photo or logo

Remember to:

- Emphasise your name, affiliation and secondary contact information
- Keep the colours simple and consistent
- Make links trackable
- Use space dividers
- Make your design mobile-friendly

Improving your email signature may not be on the top of your to-do list but remember that it's the cumulative effect of all the little things that makes the difference.

Nine Powerful Words to Use in Your Messages

Here are 9 powerful words you can use in your marketing messages

You- make it all about the customer

Free- Who can resist a free offer?

Because- Show then why they need it

Risk-free- They feel secure giving their money

Secret- Everyone wants a special tip or hack

Instantly- Promises a quick payoff

Limited- Scarcity creates a sense of urgency

Easy- No one wants to deal with hassle

Don't miss- Capitalises on fear of missing out.

You can use these in emails, on your website, in posts on social media, blog posts, videos and much more.

Give this a go and see if this works for you.

Take Daily Action

If you need more service users, and especially if your care service is losing money, you need to be taking daily action to find new users.

So, are you doing this? Check your to-do list for today.

Are there any activities on there which are going to help you get more service users?

Here are a few ideas of things you could be doing:

- Follow up on previous enquiries you have received
    - This should be your first priority. Go on, pick up the phone and call some of the people who have enquired in the last few weeks.
- Activities which could generate new enquiries
    - Can you do something every single day? If you don't know what to do, there is a checklist you can download in the Care Managers Hub.

Program your day to make sure you find the number of new service users you need.

FINDING STAFF

Do You Need More Staff?

Where are you posting your job adverts?

If you are only using sites like Indeed, you are really holding yourself back.

Social media is a great way of finding carers- most of them are young and that's where most of them are spending their time.

So get posting in Facebook, Instagram, Twitter and any other sites that you use.

Posting in your local Facebook groups is a great way of finding people.

But don't just do it just once- you need to keep repeating it until you get the success you need.

Using Marketing to Find More Staff

Marketing is not just for finding more service users.

If you need more carers (and most of us do) then you can use all the techniques used in marketing to help you find more carers.

Here are some questions to be asking before you even start to recruit:

- Who is the ideal person you are looking for? Examples- qualifications, years and type of experience, location, personality and temperament etc.

- If you could wave a magic wand, what would they be looking for? Examples- job security, being part of a team, a fair salary, a fun place to work, training etc.

- What are they afraid of? Examples- not being able to do the job, not being given regular hours etc.

- What do they want? Examples- great training, friendship, support if they are stressed etc.

- What do they need? Examples- supervision, uniform, computers, phones etc.

Once you have answered the above questions in detail, you will be in a much better position to recruit successfully. You will come across as professional; and as someone who really knows what they are doing.

Be sure that you really spend some time focussing on the personality traits in the first question. You can always train skills but it's very hard to change someone's personality if it doesn't fit in with what you are looking for.

Once you have defined the kind of person you are looking for, then you can begin the marketing to find your ideal candidates.

Find Staff on Facebook for Free

If like most of us you are looking for ways to find more staff, then read on...

Ideally if you are looking for more staff, then you want to find people who live in a certain area, right? So how to do that on Facebook?

There are Facebook Groups for every area. These have names such as 'Your Town Matters', 'Everything Your Town' or 'Your Town Community'. Substitute'Your Town' with the name of your own town or area.

Go into Facebook and then into 'Groups'. Search for those groups and then join any that are relevant to you.

Once you have joined the groups you can then post your job adverts. I would make it more of an informal post rather than a formal job advert but feel free to experiment and find out what works best for you.

THE CARE
MANAGERS HUB

The Care Managers Hub is an amazing resource for managers working in care. Whether you are working in a residential care home, domiciliary care, children's home, dementia care or somewhere else, you will find resources that will help you in the successful running of your care service.

You can join for free at www.caremanagershub.com.

Here you will find checklists, reports and tip lists that you can download and start using right away.

The main areas that are covered are:

1. 'Looking After You'- resources to help you cope with all the stresses of working in a care environment.

2. 'Find New Service Users'- it does what it says on the tin. You will find here many of the downloads mentioned in this book.

If you want even more help, you can join as a Silver member where you can access the following:

1. 'Staff Matters'- if you have ever had problems in dealing with your staff, then this section is a must for you.

2. 'Improving Business'- we help you to 'do business better'.

HELPING
YOU BEAT STRESS

If you suffer from stress, overload or overwhelm, then our 'Stress Transformation Secrets' program could be just the thing for you.

Our new program will enable you to deal with stress immediately. Whenever you notice you notice that stress is becoming a problem, you will have the tools available to deal with it.

But it's not only for you, this program will help you to spot issues with your staff and help them also.

You can find out more at *https://bit.ly/3vvnEbx*. If you are a member of the Care Managers Hub you can benefit from a 10% discount off the regular price.

ABOUT GEOFF FAIRFIELD

After qualifying as an accountant and gaining valuable experience for 13 years, I decided to start my own business which was finally sold in 2016.

I am now bringing my experience to helping care-home and home-care business prosper.

After volunteering as a Trustee for a care home in Hertfordshire, I became chairman of the home. I then made it my mission to learn as much as possible about running a care home and 'the care business' in general.

After some time, I realised that many managers in care homes and also in home-care have not had much, if any, business training. And so the Care Managers Hub was born, with the idea of helping managers in care by providing the best in resources, tips and tools to help them succeed.

As a qualified Master Practitioner in Neuro Linguistic Programming (NLP), Time Line Therapy and Hypnotherapy and, with over 50 years in business, I use the latest, leading-edge techniques to ensure that you get the maximum results in the fastest time possible.

HOW YOU CAN
WORK WITH GEOFF

If you have found any of the tips and ideas in this book useful, then I can help you further.

How would you like a one-to-one call with me, completely free of charge?

I will review what you are currently doing to gain new service users and will suggest ways you can improve your marketing that you can implement immediately.

Send me an email to *info@caremanagershub.com*, together with your name and phone number, and I will call you back to arrange a good call time with you.

I can help you fill your care home or grow your home-care business.

www.ingramcontent.com/pod-product-compliance
Lightning Source LLC
Chambersburg PA
CBHW071443210326
41597CB00020B/3916